OOPS!

An English woman, according to the *Sunday Express*, was climbing into the bathtub one afternoon when she remembered she had left some muffins in the oven. Naked, she dashed downstairs and was removing the muffins when she heard a noise at the door. Thinking it was the baker, and knowing he would come in and leave a loaf of bread on the kitchen table if she didn't answer his knock, the woman darted into the broom cupboard. A few moments later she heard the back door open and, to her eternal mortification, the sound of footsteps coming towards the cupboard. The door opened. It was the man from the gas company, come to read the meter. 'Oh,' stammered the woman, 'I was expecting the baker.' The gas man blinked, excused himself and departed ...

The Blook of Bunders

BILL BRYSON, JR.

ILLUSTRATED BY ARNIE LEVIN

SPHERE BOOKS LIMITED
30–32 Gray's Inn Road, London WC1X 8JL

First published in Great Britain by
Sphere Books Ltd 1982

Copyright © 1980, 1981, 1982 by Bill Bryson, Jr.
Illustrations copyright © 1982 by Arnie Levin
Reprinted 1982

TRADE
MARK

This book is sold subject to the condition that
it shall not, by way of trade or otherwise, be lent,
re-sold, hired out or otherwise circulated without
the publisher's prior consent in any form of
binding or cover other than that in which it is
published and without a similar condition
including this condition being imposed on the
subsequent purchaser

Printed and bound in Great Britain by
Cox & Wyman Ltd, Reading

THE BLOOK OF BUNDERS

SEE FOR YOURSELF

The chef at a hotel in Switzerland lost a finger in a meat-cutting machine and, after a little peremptory hopping around, submitted a claim to his insurance company. The company, suspecting negligence, sent one of its men to have a look for himself. He tried the machine out—and lost a finger. The chef's claim was approved.

THE GRASS IS ALWAYS GREENER

Surprised while burgling a house in Antwerp, Belgium, a thief fled out the back door, clambered over a nine-foot wall, dropped down the other side, and found himself in the city prison.

ALL THAT GLITTERS

A museum in County Durham, England, stopped displaying a Roman sesterce coin from the second-century A.D. after a nine-year-old visitor correctly identified it as a plastic token given away in a promotion by a soft-drink company.

SAME TIME, NEXT YEAR

In Bermuda in 1975 a man on a motor scooter was knocked down and killed by a taxi. Exactly a year earlier the same driver in the same taxi, carrying the same passenger, had knocked down and killed the motor-scooter rider's brother, on the same street, riding the same scooter.

LOOK BEFORE YOU LEAP

Mourners at the funeral of Anna Bochinsky in Moinesti, Rumania, were naturally somewhat taken aback when she abruptly leaped from her coffin as it was being carried to the grave. Before they could react to this unexpected outburst, the woman bounded into the nearest road, where she was run over and killed by a passing car.

REACH OUT AND TOUCH

A prison escapee in Utah surprised officials at the state penitentiary by calling them long distance "just to see how things are."

FINNEGAN'S WAKE

In 1976 a twenty-two-year-old Irishman, Bob Finnegan, was crossing the busy Falls Road in Belfast, when he was struck by a taxi and flung over its roof. The taxi drove away and, as Finnegan lay stunned in the road, another car ran into him, rolling him into the gutter. It too drove on. As a knot of gawkers gathered to examine the magnetic Irishman, a delivery van plowed through the crowd, leaving in its wake three injured bystanders and an even more battered Bob Finnegan. When a fourth vehicle came along, the crowd wisely scattered and only one person was hit—Bob Finnegan. In the space of two minutes Finnegan suffered a fractured skull, broken pelvis, broken leg, and other assorted injuries. Hospital officials said he would recover.

THEY SPARKED HIS FANCY

"I just like to see them around," a man in Denver, Colorado, explained to police after they found that his house was packed with 290,000 spark plugs that he had stolen from the factory where he worked.

MOM, BY TKO, IN THE SIXTH

Aspiring Brazilian boxer Manuel Salgado, aged seventeen, suffered a serious reversal to his career when his mother dragged him out of the ring during a bout in Rio de Janeiro and ordered him to go home and finish his homework.

FOLLOW THE NOSE

After a burglar had thrown a brick through a jewelry store window in London, police were surprised to find that nothing had been taken. In fact the would-be thief had left something behind—his nose. Apparently when heaving the brick the burglar had made the rather elementary error of standing too near the window and a falling shard of glass had neatly sliced off his outer olfactory system. Police apprehended the culprit after a brief search of nearby hospitals for recent, noseless admissions.

POLE VAULT . . .

Woodrow W. Creekmore was driving near his hometown of Chickasha, Oklahoma, in 1976 when a tie-rod on his car broke, sending the vehicle into a telephone pole. Fortunately Creekmore wasn't hurt. Unfortunately, as he was standing by the car discussing the accident with a policeman, the pole abruptly 'keeled over, striking Creekmore on the head and killing him outright.

IGNORANCE WAS BLISS

The town clerk in London, England, commissioned some efficiency experts to suggest methods for reducing municipal expenditure. After an investigation, the efficiency experts submitted a report stating that the most expedient saving could be achieved by firing the town clerk.

HIS HEART WASN'T IN IT

A woman in suburban London awoke one morning to find the dead body of a man half in and half out of her bedroom window. After a great deal of head scratching, police eventually concluded that he was a burglar who had become stuck and had suffered a fatal coronary in trying to extricate himself.

A MOVING VIOLATION?

An opportunistic thief in Cleveland, Ohio, grabbed a woman motorist's arm when she stuck it out the window to signal a left turn and stripped it of $800 worth of jewelry.

CELL BLOCKHEAD

After picking up Riso Mihail for questioning in regard to a minor motoring offense, police in Austria put him in a jail cell and then forgot about him. He languished for eighteen days without food before anyone noticed him sitting quietly in the cell growing visibly thinner. Police said Mihail was overlooked because of interdepartmental confusion, but were unable to offer any explanation for why he failed to bring his plight to their attention.

MALLFUNCTION

A seventy-eight-year-old woman in Utrecht, the Netherlands, became so hopelessly lost in a massive shopping center that she spent three days wandering around before finding her way out.

WHAT A PANE!

Thousands of windows in Manhattan were broken when a gas cylinder on a municipal truck blew up in 1978. The truck had been sent as part of a noise-abatement campaign.

LIVING IT UP

When Craig Boyden, aged thirty-two, learned he was suffering from Crohn's disease and had only three months to live, he decided—not unreasonably—to make the most of the time left to him. So when he went back to his job as a credit manager for a carpet company in Elliott City, Maryland, he embezzled $30,000 from the firm and began to lead a lavish existence—dining in the best restaurants, buying drinks for everyone in every bar he went into, throwing parties for his friends at $1,000 a shot. As the weeks passed one small thing began to nag him: instead of declining into ill heath, he felt better all the time. Deciding that a second opinion might not be a bad idea, Boyden went to another doctor, where he learned that he was suffering not from Crohn's disease but from a simple hernia. It turned out he was allergic to the gloves used by the surgeon during the initial exploratory surgery, which had led to the mistaken diagnosis. After explaining everything in court Soyster was given a suspended sentence and ordered to pay restitution at the rate of $5,000 a year.

DROWNED IN DRINK

When a man in Rada-Ljevo, Serbia, fell into a twelve-foot vat of plum brandy and began flailing about in a helpless fashion, his son dove in after him. When he too showed no evidence that he might eventually emerge, the father's wife leaped in to give a hand, but quickly joined in the helpless flailing. The son's wife, apparently not one to ignore a trend, jumped in as well, but with as little practical effect. All four drowned.

NEXT TIME, TRY CUTTING DOWN ON YOUR EXPENSES

After he was unable to open a safe he had stolen, Wiener Bryan of Rochester, New York, spent $31 in cab fares taking it around town in a futile effort to get it open before finally giving up and dumping it in the Seneca River. Wiener's reaction when he learned, after being arrested and sentenced to twenty years in jail, that the safe contained only forty-four pencils and some postage stamps was not recorded.

MY PLACE OR YOURS?

In 1955 the Frostburg, Maryland, State Teachers College basketball team arrived in Latrobe, Pennsylvania, for a game with St. Vincent's College only to find the gym locked up and in darkness. A quick telephone call revealed that the St. Vincent's team at the same time was peering in a perplexed fashion through the darkened windows of the gym in Frostburg.

OUT OF THE FRYING PAN

An American tourist in South America had the decidedly grave misfortune to be attacked by killer bees as he stood on the bank of the Amazon. Seeking refuge, he leaped into the river—and was devoured by piranha fish.

MAKING TRACKS

In a stroke of genius a burglar in Chattanooga, Tennessee, put his socks over his hands to avoid leaving fingerprints at the scene of the crime. He was arrested, however, when police identified him by his footprints.

YOU ARE WHAT YOU EAT

In Poland in the summer of 1979 a man named Henry Hendrick appeared in court and was fined for making his wife eat a loud tie she had given him as a present.

LET'S DO THIS AGAIN SOMETIME

While motorcyling through the Hungarian countryside, Cristo Falatti came up to a railway line just as the crossing gates were coming down. While he sat idling, he was joined by a farmer with a goat, which the farmer tethered to the crossing gate. A few moments later a horse and cart drew up behind Falatti, followed in short order by a man in a sports car. When the train roared through the crossing, the horse started and bit Falatti on the arm. Not a man to be trifled with, Falatti responded by punching the horse in the head. In consequence the horse's owner jumped down from his cart and began scuffling with the motocyclist. The horse, which was not up to this sort of excitement, backed away briskly, smashing the cart into the sports car. At this, the sports-car driver leaped out of his car and joined in the fray. The farmer came forward to try to pacify the three flailing men. As he did so, the crossing gates rose and his goat was strangled. At last report the insurance companies were still trying to sort out the claims.

HOT STUFF

A man in California sued the Citrus Heights Fire Department after he had given them permission to come onto his property for some much-needed honing of their skills. According to the suit the fireman let their practice fire get out of control and it burned the man's house down. Meanwhile, across the country in upstate New York, a woman watched her home go up in flames while two fire departments stood on the lawn bickering over which of them was going to tackle the blaze.

During a demonstration of airborne forest-fire control in Michigan in 1958, pilot Milton Nelson missed his burning target and instead dropped his planeload of fire-retarding liquid on the 150 onlookers.

A PENNY SAVED

In 1955 the state senate in Illinois disbanded the state's Committee on Efficiency and Economy for "reasons of efficiency and economy."

WHICH END IS UP?

In California a Huntington Beach woman received $250,000 after "an improperly administered enema" led to her suffering irreversible lung damage.

WHOSE SIDE ARE YOU ON?

While searching for Confederate raiders near Lawrenceburg, Indiana, during the Civil War, a regiment of Union militiamen galloped around a hill, spotted some soldiers riding away from them at speed, and opened fire. Five men were killed and seventeen wounded before the attacking soldiers realized they were firing on the rear of their own regiment.

•

Janos Zeklos, a professional soccer player in Rumania, decided to hang up his cleats in 1979 after accidentally scoring against his own team for the twenty-third time in his career.

SHE STARTED IT!

Alvin and Sarah Ratskeller were asleep in their home in Homewood, Illinois, early one morning when fifty-year-old Mrs. Ratskeller awoke, fetched a pistol and shot her husband twice in the chest as he slept. She then got back into bed beside him and fell asleep. Several hours later Mr. Ratskeller awoke and saw what his wife had done. Not being one to let these things pass lightly, he pulled the gun from her hand and shot her once in each leg. Not surprisingly this awoke the woman and she regained control of the gun. While her husband beat a tactical retreat on all fours into another part of the house, Mrs. Ratskeller reloaded the gun, crawled after him, and shot him in the mouth. He managed to crawl away and she then shot herself while he broke a window and called for help. When police arrived they found the resilient couple resting on the floor. As they came forward Mrs. Ratskeller raised herself and took one final shot at her husband. The shot missed, however, and she fell dead.

TAKE MY LIFE—PLEASE!

Intent on suicide, Frenchman Jacques Lefevre drove a stake into the ground on the top of a cliff overlooking the sea, then tied one end of a rope around the stake and the other around his neck. Being nothing if not thorough Lefevre then drank a bottle of poison, set his clothes on fire, lowered himself over the cliff, and tried to shoot himself in the head. Unfortunately he missed, the bullet cut the rope in two, dropping the hapless gentleman into the sea, where the salt water put out his flaming clothes and caused him to spew up the poison. A passing fisherman picked Lefevre up and delivered him to a nearby hospital, where at last the weary Frenchman got his wish—and died from the effects of exposure.

UNDER ALL

The election prospects of Jonathan Unger, a city-council candidate in Fleetwood, England, dimmed appreciably after it was discovered that he was in the habit, when out making door-to-door solicitations for votes, of stealing ladies' underpants from clotheslines.

THAT SINKING FEELING

Twenty-eight members of a weight-watching club in Australia suffered the exquisite embarrassment of having their bus sink up to its axles in a tarred parking lot during an outing.

BIG GIRLS DON'T CRY

Casey McGurr, aged sixty-two, proposed to his wife, Alice, on the strength of a lonely-hearts advertisement in which she described herself as being five feet four inches tall and weighing 118 pounds, and went ahead with the ceremony even though it turned out she actually weighed 450 pounds and stood over six feet tall. But the marriage did not last. As McGurr explained to a divorce-court judge in Baltimore: "She proved too much for me when she grabbed the kettle and scalded me and then shot at me and then left me, saying I didn't appreciate a fat woman."

THANKS FOR NOTHING

When an elderly lady's cat got caught up a tree in London in 1978, a British army unit gallantly came to her aid and rescued the animal for her. After receiving the woman's heartfelt thanks and acknowledging the applause of onlookers, the soldiers climbed into their truck and drove off—and ran over the cat as they went.

SOMETHING AFOOT

When Frenchman Jacques Perrer discoverd that an eighty-six-year-old acquaintance carried his life's savings in his socks, he murdered the elderly man and absconded with the money. Perrer was arrested a few days later, however, when a bank clerk thought some bills he was trying to pass smelled funny.

GOING MY WAY?

The day after leaving Waukesha, Wisconsin, for a vacation in Florida, Thomas Kilpatrick won first prize in a local charity draw. His prize was a vacation in Florida.

MONKEY BUSINESS

A Malaysian monkey that had been trained to gather coconuts from trees demonstrated a pressing need for a refresher course when it leaped onto the shoulders of a passerby in Kuala Lumpur and tried to twist his head off. The passerby was treated at a local hospital for a sprained neck.

TUT, TUT

When the Egyptian government agreed to send the treasures from the tomb of King Tutankhamen to Paris for an exhibition in 1966, the nation's director of antiquities, Mohammed Ibraham, fought the decision bitterly because he feared the curse of the pharoahs. The curse, as every schoolboy knows, has it that anyone who dares to move the treasures will be eternally doomed. After a final despairing meeting, at which he was overruled yet again, the unhappy Ibraham stepped out onto the streets of Cairo and was promptly run over by a car and killed.

SURPRISE PACKAGE

After saving 2,000 cigarette coupons Joseph Begley of Worcestershire, England, packaged them up neatly and mailed them off to the tobacco company with a request for a wristwatch. A few days later Mr. Begley received a golf bag, two electric blankets, a pressure cooker, a doll, some record albums, three tape recorders, some pots and pans, three wristwatches, and a number of other miscellaneous items. Mr. Begley kept one of the wristwatches, packed the other things up and dutifully sent them back. A few days later the tobacco company sent Mr. Begley 10,000 cigarette coupons by the way of gratitude for his honesty and apology for his inconvenience. With his new coupons Mr. Begley ordered some household tools and a bedspread. A few days later the company sent him two stepladders and a plant stand.

FIND THE HIDDEN WARD

In Mozambique workmen constructing an extension to a seven-year-old hospital knocked down a wall and discovered a forgotten maternity ward and about $100,000 worth of equipment. Eventually it was decided that someone had walled up the ward instead of putting in a door. Authorities planned an investigation into why no one had missed it.

CHILD'S PLAY

In Fort Lauderdale, Florida, a sixteen-year-old youth was charged with beating up his fifteen-year-old wife after the latter hid the caps to his toy pistol.

SEEING IS BELIEVING

When his .38-caliber revolver failed to fire at its intended victim during a holdup in Long Beach, California, robber James Elliot did something that can only inspire wonder: he peered down the barrel and tried the trigger again. Happily for most concerned, this time it worked.

RUBBER BARON

An Englishman whose attire required some explaining was fifty-seven-year-old bachelor Matthew Grey, whom police found in some bushes one night wearing a red rubber dress with a black rubber undersuit, a black rubber bra, a rubber cloak, long black rubber gloves, two rubber belts, a blond wig and—a truly inspired touch—a rubber bow tie. "I had had a very bad day," Mr. Grey explained.

SAME TO YOU, FELLA

Laborer Alexander Robinson of Mobile, Alabama, redefined the limits of tactlessness when he opened his eyes after surgery to restore his sight and said agreeably to his wife: "Boy, you sure have got fat in four years."

A BATTY IDEA

A fifty-six-year-old Polish man died in Stoke-on-Trent, England, after choking on a clove of garlic he had placed in his mouth overnight in an effort to ward off vampires.

IS IT SOUP YET?

Just after the Second World War, there lived in the village of Hechingen, Germany, a family named Wallishauser. Chronically short of food the members of the family eagerly awaited the food parcels sent to them by relatives in America. In one of these parcels Frau Wallishauser found a can filled with an odorless gray powder, which she took to be instant soup. She added a little semolina to give it body and all the Wallishausers agreed it was the best soup they had had since before the war. The next day the family received a letter from the relatives in America saying that they had included in the last parcel a small can filled with the ashes of their late grandmother, whose dying wish it had been to have her remains buried in German soil.

NOW THAT'S WHAT I CALL A PICKY EATER

After a high-speed chase across Indiana, a car thief explained to police that he had driven across the border into Ohio before surrendering in order to make the theft a federal offense, because he thought the food would be better in a federal prison than a state one.

"LOOK, MA—NO HANDS"

Charged with driving the getaway vehicle after a murder in New York, Domingo Osario was released when it was brought to the attention of the police that Osario had no arms.

THERE'S NO PLACE LIKE HOME

Two hours after escaping from Norwich Jail in England, Jerry Wolfson knocked on the door and asked to be let back in, muttering that he was cold and wet and had developed an embarrassing tear in his pants.

NICE RUNNING INTO YOU!

Two West German motorists had an all-too-literal head-on collision in heavy fog near the small town of Gutersloh. Each was guiding his car at a snail's pace near the center of the road. At the moment of impact their heads were both out of the side windows when they smacked together. Both men were hospitalized with severe head injuries. Their cars weren't scratched.

THAT'S USING YOUR HEAD

After a woman fainted at a check-out counter at a supermarket in Nuremberg, West Germany, it was discovered that she had been trying to smuggle a frozen chicken out of the store under her hat. She was taken to a hospital with suspected brain damage.

SKINNY DIP

The members of a scuba-diving team in Cornwall, England, decided in late 1979 to go diving in Loch Buidhe, Scotland. After acquiring the permission of the loch's owner, they loaded up their equipment, drove 700 miles, lugged their gear 3,000 feet up a mountain and discovered that Loch Buidhe is only six inches deep.

RIP VAN WHO?

In 1953, when Mrs. Alice Coe went to a mental hospital in Jamestown, Virginia, to visit her aunt, she was told the woman was dead, but that she could see her room. Feeling sleepy, Mrs. Coe lay down on her aunt's bed for a nap and when she awoke a doctor told her she was being transferred to another ward. Mrs. Coe went with him. Twenty-five years later, in 1978, the error was discovered and Mrs. Coe was released. "I am the sort of person who is inclined to let things take their natural course," Mrs. Coe explained.

IS IT HOT IN HERE OR IS IT JUST ME?

Sometime during the late night of July 1 or the early morning of July 2, 1951, Mrs. Mary Reeser, aged sixty-seven, of St. Petersburg, Florida, erupted in flames and burned up her bedroom. No one knows quite why. About all that remained of Mrs. Reeser when she was found in the morning were a small pile of smoking ash and one very shrunken skull. Experts estimated that it would have taken a fire of 3,000 degrees to have so thoroughly carbonized the woman, yet the heat had been localized to the corner of the room where she had been sitting. "Never have I seen a body so completely consumed by heat," said leading investigator Wilton Korgman, who added rather fatuously, "This is contrary to normal experiences." Mrs. Reeser was not struck by lightning. Nor did she come in contact with inflammable liquids or an electrical source. Beyond that, no one knows what happened—and at this date it's not likely anyone ever will.

•

An even more baffling case of spontaneous human combustion came in 1938 in Chelmsford, England.

Phyllis Newcombe, aged twenty-two, was dancing with her fiancé at a local gathering when in full view of several witnesses she suddenly—and irremediably—burst into flames.

BRIDGING THE GAP

When New York policeman Joseph Piotkowski spotted a man perched high up on Manhattan Bridge, he bravely risked his life to inch his way up the girders to try to talk the man into coming down. Arriving breathlessly at the top, Piotkowski asked the man what had driven him to climb up there. "It's my job, damn it," snapped the man. "I'm an inspector for the Department of Public Works."

"I ALWAYS WANTED A COMPACT CAR"

On his first assignment for a Chicago newspaper a rookie reporter drove a company car to a car-crushing plant, parked in the wrong spot, and returned from interviewing the manager in time to see the vehicle being compacted into scrap metal. It was also his last assignment for the paper.

GOOD VIBRATIONS

A postman in Le Havre, France, alerted bomb-disposal experts when he realized that a package he was about to deliver to the residence of a buxom blonde was ticking in a sinister fashion. The blushing woman brought the crisis to an abrupt end, however, when she revealed that the parcel contained a battery-operated vibrator that had somehow switched itself on.

SALAD DAZE

Called to a mobile home just outside Lakeview, Ontario, in 1958, police found the dwelling spattered with eggs and strangely quiet. One of the home's two occupants sat in a chair, his face covered with shaving cream, an egg in one hand. He was dead. The other occupant was unconscious. He had a salad bowl over his head, a sheet around his shoulders, and was dressed as a jockey. "We are holding the jockey for questioning," the police explained.

YOU ONLY DIE ONCE

When she found her husband slumped at the kitchen table after a monumental drinking spree, Bridget Schenk, aged thirty-seven, of Oldenburg, West Germany, lost her composure altogether and shot him twice in the back. This proved to be both unfortunate and unnecessary since a subsequent autopsy showed that at the time of the shooting her husband was already dead, apparently the victim of a heart attack. Frau Schenk was jailed anyway, for attempted murder.

LUCKY STRIKE?

In 1918 in Flanders, Belgium, a certain Major Summerford was struck by lightning and invalided out of the Canadian army. Six years later he was fishing in Vancouver when lightning struck him again, paralyzing his right side. Within two years he had recovered sufficiently to be walking through a local park when—you guessed it—he was struck again. This time he was paralyzed for good and, after lingering for two years, died of his injuries. There is a brief postscript: in 1934, during a thunderstorm, lightning shattered a tombstone at a Vancouver cemetery. It was Major Summerford's.

A DRIVEN MAN

Out for a spin with his wife, Thomas Basil, aged seventy-six, of Minneapolis, Kansas, crashed into a parked car, forcing it to slam into another. Pulling over to see what he had done, Basil managed to crash into a third car. He and his wife got out to survey the damage. Getting back into his car to move it out of the way Basil then hit his wife, breaking three of her bones, and ran into a building.

DIE, DIE, MY DARLING

When Norma Kroll of San Diego, California, grew peeved with her husband, she put a massive dose of LSD on his toast. When this failed to elicit any discernible response in him, she served him a blackberry pie containing the venom sac of a tarantula spider, sabotaged his truck with a rudimentary bomb, placed a live electric wire in his shower, injected air into his veins with a hypodermic syringe while he was asleep, and liberally laced his beer with tranquilizers. When all of these endeavors failed to disturb his equilibrium even slightly, Mrs. Kroll decided to abandon subtlety and hit him over the head with a steel weight. She was sentenced to life in prison.

YES, BUT CAN HE SCORE A TOUCHDOWN?

After paying Alan Gerfield total disability payments for fifteen months, the Rhode Island Workmen's Compensation Commission decided to withdraw them after it was brought to their attention that Gerfield was a member of the University of Rhode Island's football team.

GREAT PRETENDERS

When Dr. Ari Roga, a successful physician in Salzburg, Austria, baked a fancy cake for one of his patients, the woman joked that he must have had professional culinary training. As it turned out, she was right. An investigation revealed that Dr. Roga was not a doctor at all, but a pastry chef from Vienna.

Similarly, in Rome an expatriate Greek doctor came a cropper when another native Greek came to him for treatment and noticed that the impressive certificate on his wall was not, as everyone had supposed, a medical diploma, but a certificate from the Greek merchant marine.

A FAREWELL TO ARMS

In July 1979 representatives of the United States Air Force partially restored the arms balance when they reclaimed three Hawk missile launchers from the Florida premises of Walt's Auto Salvage. The missile launchers had been towed there from a public parking lot after the Air Force had parked them and then somehow contrived to forget about them.

ONE IF BY LAND

In 1972 an ambitious but not noticeably well-educated man in Argentina was arrested after trying to hijack a bus to Cuba.

NEXT TIME, TRY THE CLOSET

Heinrich Schwab found himself in a classic predicament in Vienna when his lover's husband returned home unexpectedly one afternoon. He responded in a classic manner, by grabbing his clothes and diving naked under the bed. What he had not bargained for was that the husband, a traveling salesman named Wolfgang, was not feeling himself and had decided to go straight to bed. In spite of his nakedness and discomfort Herr Schwab thought it would be more prudent to wait out the night under the bed rather than risk waking the man, who was, he knew, a large fellow with a violent temper. To his horror, however, in the morning Wolfgang showed no inclination for arising, and in fact spent the whole day in bed, reading, dozing, and watching television. Herr Schwab stayed put throughout the day and again through the long night, squeezed beneath the bed, suppressing all manner of bodily urges. On the following morning. Wolfgang at last announced that he was ready to face the world and, after dressing and kissing his wife good-bye, he departed. His thirty-nine hours ordeal over at last, a stiff Schwab dragged himself out from under the bed. A moment later the door opened. It was Wolfgang, returning for his car keys. He gave Schwab two black eyes, a split lip, and two broken teeth.

HE'S ON PINS AND NEEDLES

When Knud Jensen fell into a barberry patch in Denmark he did it in a big way. At last report doctors had removed almost 24,000 inch-long barberry thorns from him and were still counting.

". . . AND THE SERVICE WAS AWFUL!"

Passengers in the baggage claims area at John F. Kennedy Airport in New York were understandably vexed when a large suitcase on a revolving carousel partially split open and a human arm flopped out. It transpired that the arm belonged to one Audley Gibson, aged twenty-one, late of Kingston, Jamaica, who had hit on the novel notion that he could save considerably on air fare by climbing into his brother-in-law's expansive suitcase. Unfortunately he had neglected to take into account the fact that airline baggage holds are unpressurized.

YOU OUGHT TO BE IN PICTURES

While burgling a house in Memphis, Tennessee, a young thief came across a Polaroid camera, and, while examining it, managed to accidentally take his own picture. Stupidly, he left it behind. When the owner came home and found a photograph of a startled-looking young man on the floor, he gave it to the police, who were able to identify and apprehend the culprit without a great deal of difficulty.

THAT'S WHAT THE SIGN SAID

A hungry and at least fractionally intoxicated motorist in Newington, Connecticut, took the Seme Drive-In Restaurant at its word early one morning and drove in—through the front wall. Police found him fixing a snack in the kitchen.

HARD CANDY

A deliveryman in Cumberland, England, idly threw a candy bar out the window of his van. It hit a professional wrestler on the head and knocked him out. The deliveryman was fined $20.

JULIA CHILD, TAKE NOTE

Fussy eater François Lui, a Parisian nightwatch-man, killed his wife because he didn't like her cooking. He was jailed for seven years and a short while after his release he remarried. He murdered his second wife when she burned the toast.

THANK GOD IT'S FRIDAY?

Another Frenchman who took his food seriously was Vatel, Fouquet's maître d'hôtel, who committed suicide when a delivery of fish failed to arrive.

HERE, KITTY

After buying a puppy for $40 from a stranger, Bruno Alti of Milan, Italy, couldn't help wondering why the damned thing never barked. He took his pet to a veterinarian, who quickly spotted the problem and informed the none-too-perceptive Alti that what he had bought wasn't a dog, but a lion cub.

•

DROWNS IN SINK AFTER FALL OFF MOTOR-BIKE—headline in Bournemouth, England, *Evening Echo*.

IDLE CHATTER

A woman in San Diego was granted a divorce on the grounds that her husband was so cheap he made her make her own false teeth. In Cleveland, meanwhile, Mrs. Edna Hopton, a deaf mute, won a dissolution of her marriage because her husband nagged her in sign language.

YOU ASKED FOR IT

Splendid last words were those spoken by former Vice President Alben Barkley at the University of Kentucky commencement exercises in 1956. "I would rather sit at the feet of the Lord than dwell in the house of the mighty," Barkley declared. He thereupon keeled over and died.

JUST ONE MORE FOR THE ROAD

In Boston a thief who couldn't get too much of a good thing was arrested after robbing the same liquor store three times in one day.

THAT'S SERVICE WITH A SMILE

While making a discreet getaway with a suitcase full of stolen jewelry, a burglar in the Waldorf-Astoria Hotel in New York stumbled as he came down the main staircase, dropped the suitcase, and watched slack-jawed as a variety of glittering baubles spilled out. A porter and a house detective came over, helped him put the $500,000 worth of jewels back in his case, escorted him to a cab, and waved happily as he rode off.

JAWS 3

A dentist in Regensburg, West Germany, filed a $50,000 suit against a woman who panicked while he was laboring inside her mouth and bit off a substantial portion of his finger.

SPACED OUT

A man who shoveled snow for an hour to clear a space for his car during a blizzard in Chicago returned with his vehicle to find a woman had taken the space. Understandably, he shot her dead.

THREE'S A CROWD

Just after his marriage, Philip Webb, aged twenty-four, of Birmingham, England, confessed to his twenty-two-year-old bride that he had never actually gotten around to divorcing his first wife. Upon hearing this his bride burst into tears and left him. Mr. Webb thereupon learned that his first wife had divorced him without letting him know, so he wasn't a bigamist after all. At last report he was still looking for his second wife.

HELL ON WHEELS

Workers at a mining site in Utah were amusing themselves by rolling an eighteen-hundred pound road-grader tire back and forth when the tire got out of control, bounced down a hill to a road, rolled three quarters of a mile into the nearest town, bounced thirty feet in the air and demolished the second floor of a house. No one was injured.

CHANGE OF ADDRESS

After arranging to have his house torn down, Paul Davis of Alexandria, Louisiana, arrived home one afternoon to find that the demolition men had removed the front porch, most of the upstairs, and half of the roof of his neighbor's residence.

•

In Tulsa, Oklahoma, James McEachem had the unusual experience of having his house stolen. McEachem had just bought the house and was planning to move it to a nearby town. Thus it was up on blocks—apparently an irresistible temptation for at least one ambitious criminal.

"STOP THE WORLD, I WANT TO GET OFF!"

French sisters Roben Mariotto, aged seventy-eight, and Simone Yvonne, sixty-nine, decided to fly to Portland, Oregon, to see Mlle. Mariotto's daughter. After journeying from Paris to London they caught a flight to Seattle. There they had only to catch a half-hour onward flight to Portland. Unfortunately the sisters, whose grasp of English was charmingly tenuous, boarded the wrong plane. After two hours they ventured to ask the stewardess when they might expect to arrive in Portland. "Oh, I'm afraid this plane is going to London," replied the stewardess. Six hours later the plane touched down at Heathrow, from which point the two ladies started their trip all over again.

•

Another misguided tourist was German Edward Kreuz, who got off his plane during a refueling stop at Bangor, Maine, and spent four days seeing the sights before learning he wasn't in San Francisco.

•

More impressive still was Nicholas Scotti, who got off his plane during a stopover en route from San

Francisco and spent two days in New York believing he was in his native Rome. Mr. Scotti naturally was a trifle astonished at the number of English language signs he found everywhere, but these, he decided, had been put up for the benefit of the American tourists, of whom there seemed to be a remarkable plenitude. In any case, he was far more disturbed at how many of the city's historic monuments had been torn down since he had last been there. He scarcely recognized the place and couldn't find his old neighborhood at all. To be fair, Mr. Scotti might have discovered his small delusion somewhat sooner had it not been for the fact that the one person he approached for directions was a policeman who was also a native of Italy—and who answered in flawless Italian as a courtesy.

BETTER LATE THAN NEVER

Gary Miller of St. Joseph, Missouri, was asleep in his home one night in November, 1976, when fire broke out and killed him. Mr. Miller was a fireman. An uninstalled smoke detector was found in the rubble of his home, still in its package. It was ringing.

THE HOLE STORY

When gunman Harry Leone pulled a pillowcase over his head and entered a doughnut shop in California with the intention of robbing it, one small flaw in his plan became immediately evident—he had neglected to cut eyeholes in his makeshift hood. One of the patrons recognized Leone when he raised the pillowcase to see what he was doing and police apprehended him a short while later.

ALL TOGETHER NOW. . .

Every time the local lifeboat went out on call, several aged residents at an English rest home urinated in unison. An investigation revealed that the lifeboat's shortwave radio was tuned to a frequency that activated the residents' electronic bladder-emptying devices.

WHAT A DUMMY!

A thief in Nottingham, England, who was either exceptionally incompetent or desperately deprived broke a store's plate-glass front window, ignored all the merchandise, and ran off with a naked, life-sized mannequin.

. . . BUT I KNOW WHAT I LIKE

Municipal workers in Toronto, finding what they took to be discarded junk in a local park, hauled it to a dump and buried it. It turned out the junk was actually from an open-air display of modern art. Ten artists demanded compensation.

BEE THAT AS IT MAY

While traveling by train to Budapest a Hungarian bee expert discovered with alarm that some bees he had with him had escaped from their container and were crawling up his legs. Explaining his difficulties to his fellow passengers he suggested that they might wish to vacate the compartment, both for their own protection and to afford him the opportunity for a little hasty disrobing. However, as the bee expert was taking off his pants, an express train roared past and the sudden draft blew the pants out into the corridor, where they chanced to become wrapped around the head of a conductor. An onlooker pulled the emergency cord. The train screeched to a halt and somehow caught fire. Officials rushing to the source of all this excitement found the bee expert without any pants on and concluded he must be an escaped lunatic. He was bundled off to a sanitorium where it took him three days to convince doctors that his story was not just the inspired babblings of a madman.

STAY TUNED

In Yamamoto, Japan, Etsuya Kobi stole a television set after breaking into a private residence, was caught and sent to jail for a year. Upon his release Mr. Kobi returned to the same residence, stole the same television, was arrested, tried, and sent back to the same prison cell.

HE'S GOT A POINT

A man in Cleveland admitted to police that he had shot and killed his wife on his day off, but refused to answer any other questions on the grounds that what he did on his day off was his own business.

PLENTY OF BREAD, BUT NO DOUGH

In 1977, six armed men burst into a high-value cargo strongroom at London's Heathrow Airport, tied up three nightwatchmen and escaped with a packet of sandwiches.

MUSIC HATH CHARMS

When listeners to radio station WFMT in Chicago heard the end of a Busoni sonata followed by interminable scratchings of a completed record, they became concerned and phoned police. Arriving, police found disc jockey Ross Chapin, aged twenty-seven, snoring softly beside his microphone.

NOVEL NAVEL

The New York State Supreme Court awarded a forty-two-year-old businesswoman $854,000 in 1979 after a plastic surgeon accidentally moved her belly button about two inches off center during cosmetic surgery to give her a "nice flat belly."

WHO'S FOR LUNCH?

The U.S. Department of Agriculture decided to change the name of the Alferd Packer Grill in one of its buildings after it was brought to the department's attention that Alferd Packer was a Colorado prospector who was jailed in 1874 for killing and eating five people.

GIVE THE GUY A BREAK

In the five years between 1972 and 1977, Mike Maryn, aged fifty-six, of Passaic, New Jersey, was mugged eighty-three times and hospitalized at least twenty times. In the course of being hit over the head with a pipe, stabbed and shot at, he had his nose broken, his ribs fractured, his teeth knocked out, his ear partly torn off, and his skull split open and fractured. He lost more than $2,000 in cash, four cars, and countless bags of groceries. Police offered him a walkie-talkie so he could call them for help, but he declined it on the not illogical grounds that "it would only be taken from me."

GIRL ON THE REBOUND

Evidently a temperamental fellow, Parisian Byron Delair threw his girl friend out of his fourth-story apartment window. With an élan that would have impressed Errol Flynn, the girl bounced off an awning, landed on the ground on her feet, and ran back upstairs, where she concussed her astonished boyfriend with a wine bottle.

FOOD FIGHT

In a classic case of one thing leading to another, seven men aged eighteen to twenty-nine received jail sentences of three to four years in Kingston-on-Thames, England, in 1979 after a fight that started when one of the men threw a french fry at another while they stood waiting for a train.

QUIT WHILE YOU'RE AHEAD, I ALWAYS SAY

After falling seventy-five feet from chimney scaffolding in 1957, twenty-two-year-old Herschel Andrews of Cincinnati was asked what his occupation was. "Ex-steeplejack," he answered. Asked when he had left the profession, he replied: "About halfway down."

SWEET REVENGE

A bank clerk who won a sudden promotion to manager made his former boss the office boy. Enrique Marco told a Spanish labor court that his upstart ex-assistant made him copy out the local phone book by hand and sent him out to buy cigarettes. The bank was ordered to pay Marco $56,000 compensation.

•

Unhappy over an eleven dollar parking fine Thomas B. Bryant of Corning, California, was in the enviable position of being able to exact revenge. He ordered the police department to vacate its headquarters within sixty days. Mr. Bryant owned the building.

IT WAS THE LEAST SHE COULD DO

It is not altogether impossible that new bride-groom Kenneth Marcle might have had second thoughts about his marriage after his car became bogged down in sand near Holtville, California, in 1956. Leaving his bride with the car, Marcle hitchhiked into the nearest town for assistance and returned to find both car and wife missing. The next day Marcle chanced to run into his wife in another nearby town. Breezily she told him that a stranger had come along, freed the car for her, and had taken her to Mexicali, Mexico, for a night on the town.

WHAT TO DO WHEN THERE'S NOTHING TO DO

After shooting and wounding his wife and young son, Louis Pilar of Rheims, France, told police that a three-week strike by television technicians was to blame. "There was nothing to look at," he explained, "and I was bored." Fortunately his wife did not seem to mind being shot at. From her hospital bed she said: "I don't blame my husband. It really has been very boring in the evenings."

YOU WON'T HAVE JEAN-MARC TO KICK AROUND ANYMORE

Corsican soccer enthusiast Jean-Marc Luccheti averted a certain goal being scored against his team by shooting the ball in mid-air with a revolver. He was jailed for three months.

THE HIGH COST OF LIVING

Soon after being awarded about $40,000 for inventing a training device that saved Sweden's Air Force almost $8 million, Lieutenant Colonel Ivan Saevas had reason to regret this generous recognition. First the tax authorities appropriated $30,000. Then they decided to consider the award as part of Saevas's salary. This put him in a higher tax bracket, so a further $7,000 was deducted. Finally they decided that the award was liable to social security and other miscellaneous taxes and demanded $16,000 more. This left Saevas about $13,000 worse off than when he had started. A government official agreed the tax bite seemed a bit excessive and said that the case would be investigated.

THAT'S CARRYING THE JOKE TOO FAR

The editor of the Russian humor magazine *Niagi* was fired in 1979 for not being serious enough.

I'VE HEARD OF PINK ELEPHANTS, BUT. . .

Englishman Leslie Gray was sitting quietly in a pub raising his pint of Yorkshire bitter to his lips, when the window beside him crashed open in a startling explosion of glass, and a flying vacuum cleaner sailed through, whizzing past the Yorkshireman's ear and causing him to spill a not inconsiderable portion of his drink. As Mr. Gray gaped, the vacuum cleaner hung tantalizingly in the air before him a moment and then came whizzing back. Prudently, Mr. Gray ducked and it sailed out the window again without further mishap. It transpired that workmen had been clearing out a room on the floor above the pub and were throwing old furniture out a window to the yard below. When one of the workmen had heaved the vacuum cleaner, the cord had become entangled and, pendulumlike, the vacuum had swung through the window and out again. Mr. Gray was treated at a local hospital for shock.

SLOWER, HONEY, SLOWER

Felix Faure, the French president, died from exertion: his heart gave out while he was putting to use a specially designed sex chair.

DRESS FOR SUCCESS

One of the criteria by which Miss Nude U.S.A. was chosen in 1979 was "taste in clothing."

LOST HORIZON

In 1958 the Australian movie *Walk into Paradise* was released in the United States as *Walk into Hell*.

FALLEN WOMAN

When Prague housewife Vera Czermak learned that her husband had been unfaithful to her, she threw herself out of a third-story window in despair. As it happened the philandering spouse was just that moment coming up the front walk and she landed on him. Mr. Czermak was killed, his wife merely injured.

"THAT'S NO CORPSE, THAT'S MY WIFE!"

Hitting on the novel idea that he could end his wife's incessant nagging by giving her a good scare, Hungarian Jake Fen built an elaborate harness to make it look as if he had hanged himself. When his wife came home and saw him she fainted. Hearing a disturbance a neighbor came over and, finding what she thought were two corpses, seized the opportunity to loot the place. As she was leaving the room, her arms laden, the outraged and suspended Mr. Fen kicked her stoutly in the backside. This so surprised the lady that she dropped dead of a heart attack. Happily, Mr. Fen was acquitted of manslaughter and he and his wife were reconciled.

THE JOY OF SAX

Adolphe Saxe invented the saxophone. In the course of his life he also was struck on the head by a brick, swallowed a needle, fell headlong down a flight of stairs, toppled onto a burning stove, and accidentally drank sulfuric acid.

BACKWARD THINKING

Police stopped a teenage girl in Coeur d'Alene, Idaho, after complaints that a car had been going around her neighborhood in reverse for some time. The girl told police that her parents had let her use the car, but she had put too much mileage on it. "I was just trying to unwind some of it," she said.

SENTENCED TO LIFE

When bank clerk Janos Revic was jilted by his girl friend in Belgrade, Yugoslavia, he decided the only thing to do was to kill himself. So he stole a car in order to crash it into a tree, but it broke down. He stole another one, but it was too slow and scarcely dented a fender. Police came along and charged him with car theft. While being questioned Revic plunged a dagger into his chest. He recovered, however, and was sentenced to a year in jail. On the way to his cell, Revic dove through a window to the road twenty-five feet below. A snowdrift broke his fall.

•

Equally determined, but not a great deal more successful was Spaniard Paol Guerra, aged thirty-six, who threw himself in front of a passing truck, which avoided him by crashing into a wall. Pursued by the truck driver, Guerra then ran in front of another truck. It too swerved to avoid him and went off the road and down an embankment. Pursued now by two drivers the hapless Guerra leaped on a horse, prompting its owner to join in the chase, and galloped off to a bridge, where he tried to hang himself. But his pursuers caught up with him before he had any success and dragged him off to the police station.

SLEEPING ON THE JOB

When two young men with shotguns burst into a drugstore in suburban Boston, taking all the occupants hostage and demanding drugs, proprietor Henry Harmer reacted with exemplary calm. Agreeably, he rounded up some drugs for the gunmen and even got them some water to wash them down. And he watched with satisfaction as the two men quietly crumpled. One of them had been given an assortment of tranquilizers, the other some sleeping pills and four ounces of rat poison. Police came and took the gunmen away as they slumbered.

OPEN WIDE

Refreshingly incompetent was the masher in Pointoise, France, who tried—appropriately enough—to French-kiss a girl on the street. She responded by biting off his tongue.

HE'S OUT!

In Pakistan in 1977 a cricket team showed their collective displeasure with a call by beating the umpire to death with the cricket stumps.

TAKE ME HOME, COUNTRY ROAD

In a classic case of compounded errors an elderly couple in Hot Springs Village, Arkansas, took a wrong turn while driving to a restaurant near their home, tried to get back to where they were but took another wrong turn, and finally ended up near Nashville, Arkansas, sixty miles away.

L' CHAIM!

En route to his execution in York, England, in the eighteenth century, a man known only as the Saddler of Bawtry was offered the chance to stop at a certain tavern for a parting drink, as was the custom of the time. A fatalist, the Saddler declined the opportunity to delay his death and rode on to the gallows. A few moments after he was hanged, a man on a horse arrived breathlessly with a pardon from the king.

OOOPS!

A 1978 press release from a San Francisco branch of Mensa, the organization for people who have high IQs and like others to know it, contained the spellings "attornies," "recieved" and, aptly, "intelligense."

DÉJÀ VU TO YOU TOO

David Reynolds, a college student with a vivid imagination, wrote a term paper in which he described himself as being shot dead during a robbery at a motel in Hartford, Connecticut, where he worked part-time as a night clerk. A few days after he submitted the grisly literary effort, a robber came into the motel while Reynolds was working and shot him dead.

•

In a similar vein, just after Scottish author Dougal Haston finished a novel in which the main character is caught in an avalanche while skiing in Leysin, Switzerland, Haston went to Leysin and was caught in an avalanche while skiing. In the book the character survived. Haston, however, didn't.

BUNS, ANYONE?

An unidentified English woman, according to the London *Sunday Express*, was climbing into the bathtub one afternoon when she remembered she had left some muffins in the oven. Naked, she dashed downstairs and was removing the muffins when she heard a noise at the door. Thinking it was the baker, and knowing he would come in and leave a loaf of bread on the kitchen table if she didn't answer his knock, the woman darted into the broom cupboard. A few moments later she heard the back door open and, to her eternal mortification, the sound of footsteps coming toward the cupboard. The door opened. It was the man from the gas company, come to read the meter. "Oh," stammered the woman, "I was expecting the baker." The gas man blinked, excused himself and departed.

IT'S EASIER THAT WAY

Also not overwhelmingly brilliant was the bank robber in Los Angeles who told a bank clerk not to give him cash but to deposit the money in his checking account.

•

Nor gunman Edward Mandrake of Indianapolis, who was tracked down by police without a great deal of trouble after he robbed a motorist and then made the man drive him home.

WHAT A SCREAM!

In 1968 Robert Rush, an American army sergeant, was woken at six A.M. by his wife, who screamed once and then died. At the inquest it was revealed that five years earlier the woman's sister had expired in a similar manner. She had climbed out of a local swimming pool with a look of terror on her face, screamed once, and died. Autopsies on both women failed to explain their deaths.

KEEP THE CHANGE

When the U.S. Department of Health, Education and Welfare tried to pay Andrew Bavas an automatic salary increase of $1,272 in 1979, Bavas decided to turn it down on the logical, if unusual, grounds that he didn't really need it. Far from being pleased, HEW informed Bavas that his refusal to accept the money was not only unprecedented but also illegal and, presumably as a sort of shock therapy, told him he was being transferred forthwith to Philadelphia. Bavas, a researcher at Northwestern University, resigned instead.

"FOR GOD SAKE, DON'T FLUSH IT!"

In the eighteenth century in England a man whom history names only as the Gloucester Jew contrived somehow to fall into the pit of an outdoor toilet. Since it was a Saturday and therefore his Sabbath, the man earnestly refused to let anyone help him out—not, of course, that people were clamoring for the privilege. On the Sunday, however, the unfortunate man was prepared to accept some assistance, but the local authorities refused to allow anyone to provide it since it was now *their* Sabbath. So the man was forced to spend another day and night unhappily trapped. On the Monday when the townsfolk arose and went to see how he was doing, they found that the poor gentleman had expired.

CLOSE QUARTERS

A thief who tried to take the cash register from a store in Paterson, New Jersey, in 1958 was found beneath it, pinned to the floor, when employees arrived for work in the morning.

FEELING SHEEPISH

A housewife in Wales was more than a little perplexed when on her twenty-first birthday the mailman brought her a parcel containing the head of a sheep. The unusual present, it turned out, was a gift from the woman's first-grade teacher, who for fifteen years had harbored a grudge after the woman's parents had complained about her teaching methods in 1964. The teacher was fined fifty dollars.

MISSING IN ACTION

When he found that the gas tank of his car had been drained and the battery stolen, Mr. D. A. Stoddard of Atlanta, Georgia, gave a stoic sigh and went off to procure replacements. Returning, he discovered that now the two front tires were missing. Another sigh and Mr. Stoddard trudged off to find a tire dealer. A policeman then came along and, seeing the denuded automobile, concluded it had been abandoned and had it towed away. Mr. Stoddard, struggling with two tires, arrived a short while later to find his car gone altogether.

RETURN TO SENDER

After moving into a house in Pancevo, Yugoslavia, the new owner opened some shutters in front of a walled-in window and was surprised to find that unopened mail—some of it dating back ninety years—tumbled out. Mrs. Vera Aremovic told reporters that her father and grandfather, both merchants with extensive business connections throughout the Austro-Hungarian Empire, had lived in the house during the nine decades mailmen had been dropping mail through an open shutter thinking there was a glass pane behind it. Their business had failed, she said, because their customers had complained that they never answered letters.

HEALTH NUT

Eighty-one-year-old Mrs. Elvira Thomas, described by police as "a powerhouse," was charged in 1977 with beating to death her eighty-five-year-old husband in their room at a nursing home in Willits, California. "She drinks a lot of carrot juice," explained an official.

TAKE THAT, SAM BREAKSTONE

Luigi Ferrara, a prosperous Parisian grocer, was jailed for two years in 1978 for stabbing his wife to death with a wedge of cheese.

YOU'VE HEARD OF THE MAN WITHOUT A COUNTRY?

In Florida, voters in West Hollywood in 1958 elected Frank Polage mayor but at the same time declined to incorporate the community, making Polage a mayor without a city.

THE AYE HAS IT

In another outburst of electoral impetuosity, when college-student Frank Castellucio noticed that no one was running for the post of highway commissioner in New Buffalo, Michigan, he wrote his own name in on his ballot, which was enough for a landslide victory.

"LOVE THOSE HOT SUMMER NIGHTS!"

Charged with setting fire to her hotel bed a woman in Memphis, Tennessee, resolutely denied the allegation, claiming that the bed was already on fire when she got into it. The woman was fined fifty-one dollars, but whether for carelessness or stupidity wasn't specified.

"M IS FOR THE MILLION
THINGS SHE GAVE ME. . ."

A woman in Mauritania was granted a court injunction to make her husband, who was a farmer, stop using her instead of his cow to pull a plow through the fields. The husband explained that he was reluctant to use the cow because he believed his late mother was reincarnated in it. In Singapore a young bride had to go to court to force her husband to stop letting his mother sleep under their bed. And in Chicago one Allen C. Farber brought a suit against his former in-laws, claiming that his ex-wife had been cautioned by her mother not to bear Farber any children because they might look like him.

DON'T SPEND IT ALL IN ONE PLACE

Also wreaking long-term revenge was Belgian Anton Grellier, who never forgave his parents for calling him stupid as a boy. After leaving home Grellier became a wealthy businessman and would amuse himself by regularly sending his parents generous checks on which he intentionally made stupid errors so that his parents couldn't cash them.

TRIAL BY FIRE

In a curious attempt at banishing hiccups, Jack Mytton, a notorious nineteenth-century British eccentric, set his shirt on fire. Sadly, the endeavor killed him but, as he remarked just before going under: "Well, the hiccup is gone, by God."

NO NEWS IS GOOD NEWS

Yet another hiccup victim was Heinz Isecke of Hanover, West Germany, who hiccuped constantly for two years after undergoing stomach surgery. When someone took the trouble to calculate that Isecke had hiccuped thirty-six million times and then told that to the unfortunate victim, he threw himself out of his hospital window to his death.

HOW ABOUT A HAWAIIAN PUNCH?

Fearful of going to the dentist to have an aching tooth treated, Walter Hallas of Leeds, England, asked a friend to punch him in the jaw to see if that would help. The friend did. Hallas died.

UP, UP, AND AWAY

After spending many hours practicing birdcalls at home, French ornithologist Marius Giraud went into some woods to try them out and almost immediately was shot dead by a hunter.

DUTY ABOVE AND BEYOND

In 1979, after being plagued for months by a series of hoax telephone calls, authorities at a London police station were able to end the problem when a switchboard operator traced one of the calls—to an internal line. The man who had been sending police to mythical shootouts and sieges turned out to be none other than Police Constable Arthur Balkin, who had recently been awarded $400 and a great deal of praise after being brutally attacked by a gang of criminals. The calls, Balkin confessed, had been made in an effort to liven things up a little. Worse still, he admitted that his recent injuries had not come from a gang, but had been enthusiastically self-inflicted. Balkin said he had hit himself on the head and stabbed himself with a knife just to make things look good. He was jailed for six months.

MARRIAGE, AMERICAN STYLE

Dallas Sherman of Cincinnati divorced his wife, Irene, after she intentionally wrecked two of the family cars during arguments with him. They were reconciled, however, and remarried. Unhappily, they were divorced again after another little contretemps in which Irene shot Dallas twice in the chest and once in the hand. She was placed on probation and he recovered. While trying to effect another reconciliation another family fracas erupted and poor Dallas was shot yet again. He recovered and succeeded in his reconciliation. The Shermans were married for the third time in 1977.

WE'LL CROSS THAT BRIDGE
WHEN WE BUILD IT

With an impressive lack of planning coordination, the builders of a railroad between St. Louis and Jefferson City, Missouri, sent 200 passengers on an inaugural run in November 1855 and discovered only after the train failed to appear at Jefferson City that no one had gotten around to connecting the two ends of a bridge over the Gasconade River.

"I NEVER MET A MAN I DIDN'T LIKE"

An unidentified English lady arrived home one day to find her husband working beneath his car, his legs sticking out. As she passed she said, "Hello, darling," and impulsively gave him an intimate squeeze. She then proceeded into the house where, to her horror, she met her husband in the hallway. Meanwhile their next door neighbor had sustained a wound to his forehead that required three stitches.

DON'T BUG ME

While in Moscow for a concert, according to the London *Evening Standard,* pianist Artur Rubinstein carefully searched his. hotel room for electronic bugs. He found some wires under the carpet and snipped them with his scissors. The following day he learned from a chambermaid that a funny thing had happened the night before—a chandelier had fallen down in the room below his.

•

EFFECTIVE IMMEDIATELY THERE WILL BE NO PARKING AT THE NO PARKING SIGNS—Sign in Fryburg, Ohio

'TIL RICE DO US PART

A man was convicted of bigamy in Brooklyn, New York, after his wife found uncooked rice on the floor of the family car and became suspicious.

THE STING

When her house was invaded by wasps, a woman in Wellington, New Zealand, made a desperate phone call to the Department of Agriculture and was told that a circular on pest control would be put in the mail to her within a day or two.

WHAT'S IN A NAME

In 1957 the winning entry in a contest to name a club for Great Northern Railway employees was The Great Northern Railway Employees Club.

THOSE WHO CAN'T, TEACH

En route to give a lecture in Cleveland, Ohio, Lancelot Dillger pulled out of his driveway and drove straight into a delivery van. With his car incapacitated, Dillger borrowed his father's, but in hurrying to get to the lecture hall he took a corner too fast and crashed into a truck. Dillger finally arrived to give his lecture by taxi. His topic for the evening was safe driving.

DID YOU KNOW?

The first Boy Scout troop in Vermont was organized in Vermont.
> —Item in Connecticut newspaper

•

CHILE, BOLIVIA SIGN
CHILE—BOLIVIA PACT
—Headline in *Des Moines Tribune*

FIRST THINGS FIRST

In December 1979 two young men and a young woman broke into a department store in Frankfurt, West Germany, with the intention of burgling it. But as they were passing through the furniture department, the young woman and one of the young men decided to pause for a little sexual horseplay on a sofa. When the other young man asked if he might join in and was refused, he became miffed and went off to a telephone, from which he called police and told them a robbery was in progress. He then departed. Police arrived a few minutes later and arrested his frolicking colleagues.

DYING OF HUNGER

A hearse driver in Kansas City left a funeral procession in chaos by suddenly speeding away, wildly overtaking other cars, going on and off the road, and generally failing to behave with funeral decorum. When police caught up with him, the hearse driver explained that he had been overcome by an urge to get a quick bite to eat.

IT'S A GAS

Englishman John Stratton, depressed over his separation from his wife, decided to end it all. He sealed all the doors and windows of his home, turned on his oven, and waited for the worst. When, after several hours, nothing had happened, it dawned on him that his house was supplied with North Sea gas, which isn't toxic. As a result Stratton apparently decided to think things over. So he lit a cigar—and blew himself up.

WASTE NOT, WANT NOT

When Roberto Rodriguez of Pecaya, Venezuela, opened his eyes and realized he was in a coffin—and, moreover, that someone was shoveling dirt onto it—he was understandably annoyed and emerged protesting. This had an unfortunate effect on his mother-in-law, who promptly fell over dead. After a brief graveside consultation and seeing that the hole had already been dug and paid for, authorities decided to bury his mother-in-law instead—after making sure, of course, that she was quite dead.

"I DO—I THINK"

One of the least durable marriages of all time was that of Yugoslavian architect Vaclaw Brychta and his English bride, Janet. At their wedding reception in London in 1977, just two hours after exchanging vows, Vaclaw excused himself, left the room, and disappeared. "If I see him again, I could kill him," said the former Mrs. Brychta after being granted a divorce two years later.

CHOOSING SIDES

After spending two hours pleading with a deranged gunman to give himself up and come out of his house, police in Oakland, California, were able to call the siege off when they discovered that the gunman was standing beside them, shouting entreaties to himself.

•

Similarly, in East Hampton, Connecticut, a group of volunteers dragging a lake were able to cease their efforts when a man helping them realized the presumed drowning victim they were looking for was himself.

GRIN AND BEAR IT

In a novel approach to do-it-yourself dentistry, Ernesto Erosa, a farmer in Uruguay, decided to combat a nagging toothache by shooting away the offending incisor with a .22-caliber pistol. The exercise was a limited success: Erosa got the tooth all right, but also managed to blow away his lower lip, his jaw, and both gums.

•

Still on the subject of dentistry, in 1936 a dentist in New York administered a general anesthetic to a female patient and then underwent the alarming experience of having her place a stranglehold on his testicles. In spite of this assault the woman successfully sued the dentist for $500 because he broke one of her fingers in extricating himself.

TOWER OF BABEL

A mistrial was declared during the course of a murder hearing in Manitoba, Canada, in 1978, when the judge learned that one of the jurors was deaf, another spoke no English, and a third spoke no English and was deaf.

SEE NO EVIL

In spite of warning shouts from onlookers a motorist in Trenton, New Jersey, backed over a pedestrian he had just let out of his car. The motorist didn't hear the warning shouts because he was deaf. The pedestrian didn't see the car coming because he was blind.

STOP THE PRESSES

Police raiding a church near Rome in 1979 found Father Guido Antonelli, a forty-nine-year-old priest, laboring at a printing press churning out bogus 50,000 lire bills. The priest told police he had been driven to crime by a reduction in church collection.

"HEY, CAN'T YOU SEE WHERE YOU'RE GOING?"

In a not particularly convincing demonstration of extrasensory perception in 1979, English hypnotist and magician Waldo donned a blindfold, climbed behind the wheel of a car, and as television cameras recorded the event, drove straight into the back of a police van in Essex.

WHAT GOES UP. . .

When drum major Steven Harding threw his baton into the air in Ventura, California, it hit two 4,000-volt power lines, blacking out a ten-block area, putting a radio station off the air, and starting a grass fire. The baton melted.

HE DIDN'T HAVE A LEG TO STAND ON

A hunter near Mesa, Arizona, shot himself in the leg and then, in trying to summon assistance, shot himself in the other leg.

HOW'S THE WEATHER?

In 1957 a newspaper in Pasadena, California, issued this outlook: "Clear today except for early fog, followed by smog, followed by evening fog."

And in Saudi Arabia in 1979 the *Arab News* issued this admirable report: "We regret we are unable to give you the weather. We rely on weather reports from the airport, which is closed because of the weather. Whether we are able to give you the weather tomorrow depends on the weather."

THAT'S A 21-GUN SALUTE

Two police detectives in Petersburg, Virginia, were ordered to take more target practice after a restaurant they were staking out was robbed—they managed to fire twenty-one shots without hitting either of the robbers.

BIBLIOGRAPHY

The anecdotes in this book were collected over a period of about ten years from the various periodicals and books listed below. In many cases people's identities have been disguised.

AMERICAN SOURCES

The Des Moines Register and *Tribune*; the *San Francisco Chronicle*; *The New York Times*; the *Chicago Tribune*; *Newsday*, the *Los Angeles Times*; *Time*; *Esquire*; *Hustler*; *Best, Worst, and Most Unusual* by Bruce Felton and Mark Fowler (New York: Fawcett, 1975).

BRITISH SOURCES

The *News of the World*; *The Times* (of London); the (London) *Sunday Times*; the *Daily Telegraph*; the *Daily Express*; the *Sunday Express*; the *Daily Mail*; *The Guardian* (Manchester); the *Evening Standard*; the *Daily Mirror*; the *Sun*; *Titbits* magazine; *Weekend*; *Private Eye*; *Phenomena: A Book of Wonders* by John Mitchell and Robert Rickard (London: Thames and Hudson, 1977); *The English Eccentric* edited by

Harriet Bridgeman and Elizabeth Drury (London: Michael Joseph, 1975); *Cabbages and Kings: A Book of Incidental History* by Grant Uden and Roy Yglesias (London: Kestral Books, 1978); *True Stories* compiled by Christopher Logue (London: Four Square Press, 1965); *Funny, Funny, Funny* by Denys Parsons (London: Pan Books, 1976); *Funny Amusing and Funny Amazing* by Denys Parsons (London: Pan Books, 1969); *Funny Ho Ho and Funny Fantastic* by Denys Parsons (London: Pan Books, 1967); *Would You Believe It, Doctor?* by Dick and Rose Girling, et al. (London: Coronet Books, 1976).

THE COUNTRY DIARY OF AN EDWARDIAN LADY

Edith Holden

The new pocket edition of Edith Holden's bestselling THE COUNTRY DIARY OF AN EDWARDIAN LADY has all the charm and natural beauty of the first edition. This beautiful book not only makes an ideal gift, but is also now compact enough to take on country rambles so that you too can enjoy nature as the author herself did at the height of the Edwardian era.

AUTOBIOGRAPHY   0 7221 0580 0   £4.50

A selection of bestsellers from SPHERE

FICTION

NIGHT PROBE!	Clive Cussler	£1.95 ☐
CHIMERA	Stephen Gallagher	£1.75 ☐
MURDER ON CAPITOL HILL	Margaret Truman	£1.75 ☐
PALOMINO	Danielle Steel	£1.75 ☐
CALIFORNIA DREAMERS	Norman Bogner	£1.75 ☐

FILM & TV TIE-INS'

SHARKY'S MACHINE	William Diehl	£1.75 ☐
FIREFOX	Craig Thomas	£1.75 ☐
GREASE 2	William Rotsler	£1.25 ☐

NON-FICTION

TOM PILGRIM: AUTOBIOGRAPHY OF A SPIRITUALIST HEALER	Tom Pilgrim	£1.50 ☐
YOUR CHILD AND THE ZODIAC	Teri King	£1.50 ☐
THE SURVIVOR	Jack Eisner	£1.75 ☐
THE COUNTRY DIARY OF AN EDWARDIAN LADY	Edith Holden	£4.50 ☐

All Sphere books are available at your local bookshop or newsagent, or can be ordered direct from the publisher. Just tick the titles you want and fill in the form below.

Name _____

Address _____

Write to Sphere Books, Cash Sales Department, P.O. Box 11, Falmouth, Cornwall TR10 9EN

Please enclose a cheque or postal order to the value of the cover price plus:

UK: 45p for the first book, 20p for the second book and 14p for each additional book ordered to a maximum charge of £1.63.

OVERSEAS: 75p for the first book plus 21p per copy for each additional book.

BFPO & EIRE: 45p for the first book, 20p for the second book plus 14p per copy for the next 7 books, thereafter 8p per book.

Sphere Books reserve the right to show new retail prices on covers which may differ from those previously advertised in the text or elsewhere, and to increase postal rates in accordance with the PO.